The Norwich School of Painters

1. (overleaf). John Crome (1768–1821): *The Poringland
Oak*. 1818 or earlier. Oil on canvas, 125.1 × 100.3 cm.
(49$\frac{1}{4}$ × 39$\frac{1}{2}$ in.) London, Tate Gallery

The Norwich School of Painters

1803–1833

Andrew Hemingway

Phaidon · Oxford

Acknowledgements

Like all writers on the Norwich School, I have depended very heavily on the mass of documentary material painstakingly collected by James Reeve, Curator of the Norwich Museum from 1851 to 1910. I also owe a great deal to some of the writers whose publications are listed in the Bibliography. I should like to thank the staffs of the many museums, galleries and libraries who have helped me, and in particular those of Birmingham City Art Gallery; the British Library and Manuscript Room; the British Museum Print Room; the Fitzwilliam Museum, Cambridge; Trinity College Library, Cambridge; the University Library, Cambridge; the Royal Museum, Canterbury; Leeds City Art Gallery; the Friends' House Library, London; Manchester City Art Gallery; the Whitworth Art Gallery, Manchester; the Metropolitan Museum of Art, New York; the Norfolk Record Office; Norwich Castle Museum; Norwich Local History Library; the Castle Museum, Nottingham; Philadelphia Museum of Art; the Tate Gallery; and the Yale Center for Studies in British Art. Sir Edmund Bacon, K.B.E., T.D., Mr Christopher Barker and Mr Quintin Gurney also generously helped me with my inquiries.

I am extremely grateful to Dr Miklos Rajnai and Ms Marjorie Allthorpe-Guyton for the many valuable conversations I have had with them. Dr Michael Pidgley has consistently given me most useful information and advice. It was the lectures and publications of John Gage which first awakened my interest in British landscape painting, and they have remained a continuing stimulus to me.

Phaidon Press Limited, Littlegate House,
St Ebbe's Street, Oxford

First published 1979
Published in the United States of America
by E. P. Dutton, New York
©1979 Phaidon Press Limited
All rights reserved

ISBN 0 7148 2001 6
Library of Congress Catalog Card Number: 79-64174

Printed in Great Britain by Waterlow (Dunstable) Ltd.

List of Plates

Select Bibliography

Romantic landscape painting
HARDIE, Martin. *Water-colour Painting in Britain*. Vol. II. London 1966
NORWICH CASTLE MUSEUM. *A Decade of English Naturalism, 1810-1820*. Exhibition catalogue by John Gage. Norwich 1969
TATE GALLERY. *Landscape in Britain c. 1750-1850*. Catalogue by Leslie Parris and Conal Shields. London 1974
Provincial art
BRISTOL CITY ART GALLERY. *The Bristol School of Artists*. Exhibition catalogue by Francis Greenacre. Bristol 1973
FAWCETT, Trevor. *The Rise of English Provincial Art 1800-1830*. Oxford 1974
The Norwich background: history. personalities. topography.
BARTELL, Edmund. *Cromer, considered as a Watering Place*. London 1806
CHAMBERS, John. *A General History of the County of Norfolk, intended to convey all the Information of a Norfolk Tour*. Norwich & London 1829
COTMAN, Alec, & HAWCROFT, Francis. *Old Norwich*. Norwich 1961
DARROCH, Elizabeth, & TAYLOR, Barry. *A Bibliography of Norfolk History*. Norwich 1975
JEWSON, C. B. *The Jacobin City, A Portrait of Norwich 1788-1802*. Glasgow & London 1975
MUNBY, A. N. L. *The Cult of the Autograph Letter in England*. London 1962. Contains the most comprehensive account of Dawson Turner
ROBBERDS, J. W. *Scenery of the Rivers of Norfolk, from Pictures painted by James Stark*. Norwich & London 1834
ROBBERDS, J. W. *Life and Writings of the Late Wm. Taylor of Norwich*. London 1843
TAYLOR, William. *Collective Works of the Late Dr. Sayers*. Norwich 1823
TAYLOR, William. 'Outlines of a Discourse on the History and Theory of Prospect-Painting', *Monthly Magazine*, xxxvii & xxxviii, 1814
The Norwich School, general studies
CLIFFORD, Derek. *Water-Colours of the Norwich School*. London 1965
DICKES, William Frederick. *The Norwich School of Painting*. London & Norwich 1905
FAWCETT, Trevor. 'Eighteenth-century art in Norwich', *Walpole Society*, xlvi, 1976-8
RAJNAI, Miklos. *The Norwich Society of Artists 1805-1833*. Norwich 1976
REDGRAVE, Richard & Samuel. *A Century of British Painters*, chapter xxv. Oxford 1947
The Norwich School, individual artists
ALLTHORPE-GUYTON, Marjorie. *Henry Bright 1810-1873*. Catalogue of Paintings and Drawings in Norwich Castle Museum. Norwich 1973
ALLTHORPE-GUYTON, Marjorie. *John Thirtle 1777-1839*. Catalogue of Drawings in Norwich Castle Museum. Norwich 1977
ARTS COUNCIL. *John Crome 1768-1821*. Exhibition catalogue by Francis Hawcroft. London 1968
Burlington Magazine. Cotman Centenary Number, lxxxi, July 1942
CLIFFORD, Derek & Timothy. *John Crome*. London 1968
CLIFFORD, Timothy. 'John Crome's *Steam Packet*', *The Connoisseur*, clxxxv, March 1974
FAWCETT, Trevor. 'Thorpe Water Frolic', *Norfolk Archaeology*, xxxvi, 1977
GAGE, John. 'Documents of Crome and Cotman', *Burlington Magazine*, cxi, April 1969
GOLDBERG, Norman L. *John Crome the Elder*. Oxford 1978
HAWCROFT, Francis. 'John Crome and the Yarmouth Water Frolic', *Burlington Magazine*, ci, July/August 1959
HAWCROFT, Francis. 'Crome and his Patron: Thomas Harvey of Catton', *The Connoisseur*, cxliv, December 1959
HEMINGWAY, Andrew. 'John Thirtle at Norwich', *Burlington Magazine*, cxix, August 1977
HEMINGWAY, Andrew. 'Cotman's *Architectural Antiquities of Normandy*: Some amendments to Kitson's account', *Walpole Society*, xlvi, 1976-8
ISHERWOOD KAY, H. 'John Sell Cotman's Letters from Normandy 1817-1820', *Walpole Society*, xiv & xv, 1926 & 1927
KITSON, Sydney D. *The Life of John Sell Cotman*. London 1937
OPPÉ, Paul. *The Water Colour Drawings of John Sell Cotman*. London 1923
PIDGLEY, Michael. 'Cornelius Varley, Cotman, and the Graphic Telescope', *Burlington Magazine*, cxiv, November 1972
PIDGLEY, Michael. 'Cotman in Normandy', *Burlington Magazine*, cxvii, August 1975
PIDGLEY, Michael. 'Cotman's Patrons and the Romantic Subject Picture'. Unpublished Ph.D. thesis, University of East Anglia 1975
POPHAM, A. E. 'The Etchings of John Sell Cotman', *Print Collector's Quarterly*. October 1922
RAJNAI, Miklos. 'John Crome's Windmill', *Norfolk Archaeology*, xxxiv, 1969
RAJNAI, Miklos, & ALLTHORPE-GUYTON, Marjorie. *John Sell Cotman, Normandy*. Catalogue of Drawings in Norwich Castle Museum. Norwich 1975
R.I.B.A. *Architectural Drawings and Watercolours by John Sell Cotman*. Exhibition catalogue by Paul Oppé, London 1939
THISTLETHWAITE, Jane. 'The etchings of E. T. Daniell', *Norfolk Archaeology*, xxxvi, 1974

The Norwich School of Painters

In 1812, Andrew Robertson, a distinguished miniaturist and friend of Constable, visited Norwich, and in a letter written during his stay there he remarked:

I arrived here a week ago and find it a place where the arts are very much cultivated ... some branches of knowledge, chemistry, botany, etc, are carried to a great length. General literature seems to be pursued with an ardour which is astonishing when we consider that it does not contain a university, and is merely a manufacturing town.

To judge from other letters of the period, many visitors to the city were equally impressed by its vitality. The violence of its politics was notorious, and in the 1790s it was such a hot-bed of radicalism that Pitt's friends dubbed it 'the Jacobin city'. One of the leading radicals, William Taylor, was a well-known periodical writer, and an ardent partisan of modern German literature, whose translations were well regarded by the Romantic poets. Taylor was probably the city's foremost intellectual, although he himself gave the title to his friend, the poet and antiquary, Frank Sayers. Taylor described Sayers's *Dramatic Sketches of Northern Mythology* (1790) as an 'imperishable monument of English poetry', but even he had to admit that it was received by the public with 'gratitude and admiration' rather than 'eagerness and enthusiasm'. Norwich was also the home of Amelia Opie, noted bluestocking, wife of the painter John Opie, and author of the successful novel *Father and Daughter* (1801).

From the 1780s on, the city had a whole succession of clubs and societies such as the Speculative Society and the Philosophical Society, through which middle-class people met together to discuss subjects ranging from contemporary political events to abstract moral and aesthetic problems. It was a time when amateurs still made valuable contributions to many fields of knowledge. A number of Norwich antiquaries published essays on Gothic architecture, and botany too was seriously studied, perhaps partly owing to the presence of Sir James Edward Smith, first president of the Linnaean Society. Many amateurs had more than one interest, although few took their hobbies as seriously as the energetic polymath Dawson Turner, an important patron of the Norwich artists, who wrote on art, architecture, botany and travel, and still found time to run a flourishing banking business at nearby Yarmouth.

The general enthusiasm for the arts made it possible for Norwich to support a large number of artists, who earned a living mainly by teaching drawing and picture dealing, although they also undertook more menial tasks. After commenting warmly on the quality of music in the city, Andrew Robertson continued his letter:

Painting and Drawing are as much esteemed, and many are nearly as great proficients. . . . The studies of landscape about the town are infinitely beautiful and inexhaustible. The buildings, cottages, etc are charming, and have invited people to the general practise of drawing, or rather painting in water-colours from nature, assisted by a man of considerable abilities as a teacher and landscape painter. . . .

In 1803, a group of these artists and amateurs had founded the Norwich Society of Artists, and through evening meetings, exhibitions, and sketching parties, they established a sense of collective identity which makes it possible to regard them as a school. Most of the artists were landscapists, most were local-born, and they drew common inspiration from the surrounding scenery and its associations. Although they developed no common style and were very receptive to the influence of London-based artists, they did influence each other. Some of the Norwich artists took professional pupils, and most taught a wide circle of amateurs, who usually followed their style.

In 1803, the foremost artists working in Norwich were John Crome, Robert Ladbrooke, Robert Dixon, John Thirtle and Charles Hodgson. Although John Sell Cotman did not return to settle in the city until 1806, he belongs to the same generation. Crome, Ladbrooke, Hodgson and Cotman all had sons who followed the same profession, and Crome and Ladbrooke took apprentices. These formed a second generation, which included John Berney Crome, James Stark, George Vincent, Joseph Stannard, and Miles Edmund Cotman among others. A third group which included Alfred Stannard, Henry Bright and John Middleton learnt from both the first and second generations, as did three extremely talented amateurs: E. T. Daniell, Robert Leman and Thomas Lound. Although it is possible to see paintings from as late as the 1880s as productions of the Norwich School, the most vital phase of Norwich art was over by 1833, and this book is thus mainly concerned with the relationships between

artists of the first generation, and their influence on the leading figures of the second.

Norwich artists both contributed to the intellectual life of the city and benefited from it. Several of them were involved in the theatre and in musical events, and many published illustrations of architectural topography which found a market with local antiquaries. John Crome and John Berney Crome were both members of the Philosophical Society, to which William Taylor and a number of other local luminaries belonged. John Berney Crome delivered a lecture to the Society on the theme of painting and poetry which still survives, and at least three other Norwich artists gave public lectures on occasion. In turn, both Taylor and Sayers wrote on the Fine Arts. Sayers, who is said to have been an early patron of John Crome, spoke to the Speculative Society in 1791 on the question 'In what does Beauty consist?', and his paper was subsequently published in three editions. In 1814, Taylor delivered a lecture on landscape painting to the Philosophical Society, which was printed in the *Monthly Magazine* that year, and in which he claimed that architecture and townscape were the highest subjects for the landscapist while the rustic scene was the lowest—a thesis perhaps calculated to provoke Crome, whose subjects were usually of rustic type. But if Taylor was not an enthusiast for picturesque scenery Sir James Smith certainly was, and in 1810 he published a lavish folio volume illustrated with aquatints after drawings by John Warwick Smith, describing a visit to the celebrated picturesque estate at Hafod in South Wales. Although none of these men were important patrons of Norwich art some of their friends were, and together they helped to create an atmosphere sympathetic to almost any kind of intellectual and artistic activity.

The Norwich Society of Artists in some ways resembles the evening Sketching Club founded in London by Thomas Girtin, Louis Francia and five other young artists in 1799. From 1802 to 1804 John Sell Cotman played a leading role in either this club or another modelled on it, and perhaps reports of those pleasant evenings of discussion and mutual criticism inspired the Norwich artists to organize similar occasions. In any case, such gatherings of artists and amateurs were quite common in the provinces, and in Bristol at the beginning of the century a circle formed around the artist Edward Bird, which also developed a sense of collective identity through sketching parties and evening gatherings.

According to Chambers's *Norfolk Tour* (1829), the Norwich Society met in a room built for the purpose in Little Cockey Lane. No exhibition was held in the first two years of its existence, and it was probably established in the first place as a club. The members met in the evening once a fortnight, and each member had the right to suggest a subject for discussion at the following meeting. The room was available as an academy at all times on application to the president, and a collection of books, prints, casts and works of art by the members seems to have been built up.

In 1805 the Society held its first exhibition in the large room at Sir Benjamin Wrenche's Court off Little London Street. Exhibitions were then held annually until 1833, except for a two-year break in 1826–7, when the society underwent a financial crisis and moved to new rooms. They were timed to coincide with the Summer Assize Week, when many people came into the city from the surrounding neighbourhood and other amusements also took place.

Of the sixteen known members of the Norwich Society in 1806, the first year in which members are distinguished in the catalogue, five were drawing masters, one was an engraver and two were architects, so at least eight of the exhibitors could be described as professional artists if we include the two architects. The Society had three main officers: President, Vice President, and Secretary, who seem to have been elected annually. While the architects and amateurs sometimes held these offices, the record of their occupancy suggests that the organization was dominated by the drawing masters, and in this respect the Norwich Society differed from other provincial societies which were often run by local gentlemen and amateurs. The place of artists in such organizations could be a controversial issue in the early nineteenth century, and in Norwich a quarrel which was partly over the role of amateurs in the running of the Society led to a group of members seceding to organize a separate exhibition in the years 1816–18. Nearly every professional artist resident in the city exhibited with the Society, but a few, such as Henry Ninham and Joseph Stannard, never became members. Strangely, neither did two of the most talented amateurs, Robert Leman and Thomas Lound, and they also showed comparatively few works. Later Norwich exhibitions such as those of the Norfolk and Norwich Art Union (1839), the East of England Art Union (1842), and the Norfolk and Norwich Association for the Promotion of the Fine Arts (1848–55) were run mainly by gentlemen and amateurs.

From the beginning, Norwich citizens seem to have felt proud that their city had been the first to establish regular exhibitions outside London, although after the mid-1820s there were repeated complaints that they failed to give the artists much material encouragement. While the Norwich exhibitions were only the first in a whole wave of provincial exhibitions, they were unique in the extent to which the work of local-born artists predominated. Norwich certainly produced more significant painters than any other provincial city, but it was not the only place to have a school.

The central figure in the Norwich School was John Crome, although his work did not receive particularly marked attention in the Norwich press until a few years before his death. In 1820 the *Norwich Mercury* wrote that he might 'almost be said to be the father of the art in Norwich', and in 1822 described him as the founder of the Norwich School. He was born in 1768, the son of a journeyman weaver who also kept an alehouse, and after a period as an errand boy to the distinguished Dr Rigby served an apprenticeship with a coach and sign painter. By about 1790 Crome had been taken up by Thomas Harvey, a rich master weaver who lived in some style at Catton outside Norwich. Harvey was an enthusiastic amateur artist who owned an important collection of old and modern masters from which Crome studied. Crome's second mentor was the portraitist William Beechey, whom he may have met at Harvey's house. Beechey was resident in Norwich in 1783–7 and made frequent visits to the city in later years. He seems to have given Crome some instruction and Crome also visited his London studio. An acquaintance whom Crome met slightly later, about 1798, was the portraitist John Opie, who married Amelia Alderson in that year, and who is also said to have helped him.

To judge from his five surviving letters, Crome's education was fairly rudimentary, but he was witty, convivial and a good conversationalist, qualities which helped him to build up the most successful teaching practice in a city overstocked with drawing masters, and to become an intimate of several great families such as the Gurneys of Earlham. Despite early pious biography, which painted him as an example of industry and virtue, he seems to have been somewhat extravagant and partial to good living. In 1815 one local lady described him as a 'great rascal', and he seems to have had a certain independence of

outlook since he was a Freemason, a member of a Baptist Church, and recorded himself as a Liberal voter. Perhaps he sympathized with the democratic opinions which the Opies and the Gurney girls professed in the 1790s.

Before the setting up of the Secession exhibition in 1816, Crome had exhibited more works in Norwich than any other artist, but his friend Robert Ladbrooke had shown only a few less. Ladbrooke was born in 1769, and was apprenticed to a printer and engraver. About 1790 he and Crome are said to have hired a garret together and set up a business painting signboards and other ephemera. In 1793 Ladbrooke married the sister of Phoebe Berney, the girl Crome had married the year before, so that their families were linked by marriage. They quarrelled over the Secession and were reconciled only when Crome was on his deathbed. According to one of his obituaries, Ladbrooke was 'respected by all who had occasion to know him', but Dawson Turner once wrote that he was 'most dissimilar in disposition' to Crome, and he evidently lacked the charm and gaiety of his friend. It is likely that as Crome's talent outstripped his own personal jealousies obtruded between them.

Ladbrooke's son Henry once wrote that 'as a man of genius Cotman was much Crome's superior', and it is easy to believe from his many brilliant letters that Cotman's vital and unstable personality would have outshone those around him. Until his return to Norwich in late 1806 Cotman had seemed set for an outstanding career. Born in 1782, the son of a wig-maker and barber, he attended the Norwich Grammar School and received a much sounder education than Crome. He went to London in 1798 and in 1799 began to attend the evening academy at the house of Dr Thomas Monro, physician to the Bethlem Hospital, where Turner and Girtin had also worked. In 1800 he exhibited six drawings at the Royal Academy and in the same year was awarded a silver palette by the Royal Society of Arts for a drawing of a mill. He became an important figure in the Sketching Club and in the circle of young landscapists associated with John Varley. In a letter of 1802 Andrew Robertson classed him along with Turner and Girtin as one of the leading watercolourists of the day.

By 1806 Cotman had produced some of his finest work, and it is hard to understand why he decided to return to Norwich. He does seem to have had a hard time in the previous winter and he may have intended to spend a brief period there to develop his talents as a painter in oil before making a fresh assault on the metropolis. Whatever the reason, he became stuck in Norfolk for the best part of his life, and unable to narrow his horizons, he developed an acute sense of frustrated ambition. Although he spent the years 1810–22 in a remarkable attempt to establish himself as an antiquarian draughtsman and publicist, he ultimately ended up a provincial drawing master, 'the one thing I most dreaded on setting out in life'. For many years he inevitably saw the Crome family as his rivals, but he came to admire John Berney Crome and collaborated with him in the struggle to keep the Society of Artists going in the late 1820s and early 1830s.

Obviously the arrival of this outgoing young genius in 1806 must have stimulated the Norwich artists to fresh efforts. The two on whom he probably had most influence were Robert Dixon (1780–1815) and John Thirtle (1777–1839), both of whom were natives of the city. Dixon was a distinguished scene painter who worked at the Norwich Theatre, a popular drawing master and a capable watercolourist. Thirtle, the son of a shoemaker, is said to have learnt the trade of frame-making in London before returning to settle in Norwich about 1800, where he sup-

ported himself as a carver and gilder, as a miniaturist and as a teacher of drawing. Although he was Cotman's brother-in-law, Thirtle is hardly mentioned in Cotman's voluminous correspondence and he remains a very elusive personality. His work was greatly admired in Norwich where he had a considerable influence on later artists, but he exhibited outside the city on only one occasion. After the Secession, in which he played a leading role, he stopped exhibiting and was little involved in Norwich art.

*

Since Crome was seen by many of his contemporaries as the founder of the Norwich School, some account of his early work seems a necessary preface to any discussion of the group. Accounts of Crome are inevitably bedevilled by problems of attribution due to the many copies, forgeries and works by other artists which have gone under his name. The histories of his genuine pictures are often obscure, or at least it is hard to date them or relate them to his recorded exhibits with any certainty, and consequently much of what follows is necessarily somewhat conjectural.

Hardly any of Crome's work from earlier than 1805 has survived, but we know from the catalogue to a memorial exhibition of 1821 that his first sketch in oil dated from 1790 and that in 1796 he had painted compositions in the style of the great eighteenth-century landscapist Richard Wilson. Wilson's reputation was rising in the 1790s, and Turner and Girtin were also influenced by his work around that time. Crome's friend Harvey owned several pictures by Wilson, Beechey had known the artist personally, and Opie was to praise him very highly in his Royal Academy lectures, so all in all Crome's interest in this painter was more than coincidental.

2. John Crome (1768–1821): *Carrow Abbey, Norwich.*
Exhibited 1805? Oil on canvas, 133.7 × 99 cm.
(52⅝ × 39 in.) Norwich, Castle Museum

Wilson's work was particularly admired for its 'breadth', a quality Crome recommended most strongly to his pupil James Stark in a famous letter of 1816. 'Breadth' implied both the suppression of detail and the creation of pictorial effect through the arrangement of light, shade and colour in a discernible compositional structure, and academic theorists generally accepted that it could give interest even to humble subject-matter of the type preferred by Crome and the seventeenth-century Dutch landscapists. In his lecture on Painting and Poetry, Crome's son put great emphasis on the importance of breadth as a means of dignifying representations of ordinary scenery, and in this he was at one with Constable. From the beginning Crome's paintings show him very much concerned with breadth, although the means by which he tried to achieve it changed as his style developed.

The earliest oil paintings which can be firmly attributed to Crome are *Carrow Abbey* (Plate 2), the Tate Gallery's *Slate Quarries* and the *Scene in Cumberland* in the National Gallery of Scotland. *Slate Quarries* has a structure reminiscent of some of Wilson's Welsh views, while the other two resemble Wilson's work in their bold and broad handling. The sombre colouring and unnatural lighting of these pictures is unlike Wilson's, but can be compared with that of Turner's early Wilsonian paintings such as *Dolbadern Castle* (Royal Academy, exhibited 1800), and they already show that lack of finish for which Crome, like Turner, was to be repeatedly criticized. According to Allan Cunningham, the earliest writer on Crome, Beechey advised the young artist on the management of light and shade, and it is possible to see affinities between Crome's early works and the generalized landscape backgrounds of portraitists such as Beechey and Opie.

3. John Crome (1768–1821): *Whitlingham. c.* 1803–8.
Grey wash, 27.6 × 44.5 cm. (10⅞ × 17½ in.) Norwich, Castle Museum

Although the titles of exhibits in the Norwich Society catalogues indicate that Crome was probably sketching in oil outdoors by 1805 and was certainly doing so by 1807, very few of his early sketches have survived. In any case, outdoor sketching did not lead him to a naturalistic style of lighting or to bright colouring. Crome's posthumous sale included landscape sketches by Beechey, Opie and Reynolds, and like Reynolds he probably sketched in subdued colours and concentrated on chiaroscuro. Of the watercolours made on the spot which date from this time, a number such as *Whitlingham* (Plate 3) are mono-chromes, and those which are coloured are in muted tones and show no concern with light and atmosphere. What the sketches do show is Crome's remarkable ability to isolate a pictorial motive in the landscape, one of the most distinctive features of his work. None of the early oil or watercolour sketches can be related to finished pictures in either medium, but since so little of Crome's work from this period has survived it would be unwise to make any assumptions about his working process.

Like the sketches, Crome's finished water-colours from circa 1800–7 such as the British

4. John Crome (1768–1821): *View from King's Head Gardens at Thorpe*. Signed and dated July 3rd, 1806.
Pencil drawing, 15.9 × 29.8 cm. (6¼ × 11¾ in.) London, British Museum

Museum's famous *Hollow Road* are painted in broad strokes of wash which show that Crome had absorbed the influence of Girtin, but translated it into a less elegant idiom. Such drawings have the same primitive vigour as *Slate Quarries*, and must have seemed very unfinished to the artist's contemporaries. His pencil drawings at this time were equally unstylized. The *View from King's Head Gardens at Thorpe* (Plate 4) belongs to a group of four drawings which can be associated with the year 1806; it was a study for a painting now in Norwich Castle Museum. The style of this group derives ultimately from Gainsborough, and is somewhat comparable with that of Thomas Harvey's drawings.

At this point it would be desirable to compare Crome's early work with that of Ladbrooke, to see how far their developments were related. This is hardly possible. If our knowledge of Crome is based on a fragment of his output, with Ladbrooke we do not even have enough pictures to form any real conception of his development. Presumably his work was less sought after than Crome's, and he seems to have dissipated some of his energies in copying. His son Henry recorded that he was regarded as the best copyist in East Anglia, and a number of his pictures 'in the style' of other artists are listed in the Norwich Society catalogues. In 1818 the *Norwich Mercury* commented on his work in the Secession exhibition: 'He has painted so variously and so well that he may fairly challenge competition. His pictures in the manner of Claude and Poussin are particularly excellent.' In the same year the *Norfolk Chronicle* made similar remarks. None of these pastiches has been identified, but a copy by Ladbrooke after one of Wilson's Italianate pictures has survived.

Although Ladbrooke's work thus seems to have become more academic than Crome's by the time of the Secession, there is some reason to think that their early developments were related, and in the years up to 1813 they exhibited many pictures of the same subjects. In the Norwich Castle Museum there is a dark and primitive moonlight view of Yarmouth Harbour by Ladbrooke, which must be from early in his career. It is painted in very thin bituminous paint with impastoed highlights, a technique comparable with that of some pictures by Crome from circa 1805–10. The same collection also contains an equally dark landscape sketch, which is probably slightly later in date and which suggests the influence of Gainsborough. This sketch may well have been made on the spot, and the Norwich Society catalogues show that Ladbrooke was sketching in oil out of doors at least by 1809 if not before. Some further idea of Ladbrooke's work at this time can be gained from four aquatints after views of Norwich by him. These were made by S. Alken, and one of them is dated 1806. As compositions all of them are far less sophisticated than contemporary works by Crome.

While enough paintings can be attributed to Ladbrooke to make the identification of further works possible, of his drawings and watercolours virtually nothing seems to survive. This is strange considering that his watercolours received favourable comment along with those of Crome, Dixon and Thirtle in the *Norwich Mercury* in 1809, although those that do survive are unimpressive. A large drawing at Norwich, *Glymeriffe Bridge, North Wales*, is probably by him and is comparable with early drawings by Crome of Tintern Abbey. A later watercolour of Bishopsgate Bridge, traditionally attributed to him, is very carefully finished, somewhat naïve and essentially pedestrian. His few surviving pencil drawings show him to have been a much weaker draughtsman than Crome.

Over the years 1805–14, Crome was to combine his ability in isolating pictorial motives with a new command of light and atmosphere, based partly on the study of earlier painters such as Gainsborough, Van Goyen, Hobbema and Ruisdael. The study of Gainsborough showed Crome how to achieve atmospheric unity through the use of extremely fluid oil paint applied almost like a wash, and varied with areas of impastoed colour, a technique which enabled him to achieve the powerful romantic effects of the Mellon Collection's *Woodland Landscape* (Plate 5) and other works from this time. The new technique could be applied to a Dutch-inspired composition as in the Tate Gallery's *Moonlight on the Yare*, or to a theme inspired by Gainsborough himself, as in the Philadelphia Museum's *Blacksmith's Shop*. Probably Crome's latest production in this manner was the Victoria and Albert Museum's *Skirts of the Forest*, an exquisite picture, which shows him trying to convey natural effects of light and atmosphere which Gainsborough had never sought, and in which the handling of trees and foliage foreshadows Constable's in *The Haywain* of about ten years later.

In the first decade of the nineteenth century, painters such as Turner, Callcott and Havell had begun exhibiting increasingly naturalistic English views, compared with which the dramatic light effects of Crome's early pictures must have looked rather artificial. By 1810–12, Crome had developed a far more naturalistic style partly inspired by the seventeenth-century Dutch painters, as can be seen in the Castle Museum's *Yarmouth Jetty* (Plate 7). This picture is far more solid in technique

5. John Crome (1768-1821). *Woodland Landscape. c.* 1805-10.
Oil on canvas, 97.5 × 122.5 cm. (34½ × 48¼ in.)
New Haven, Connecticut, Yale Center for British Art, Paul Mellon Collection

than any of those I have discussed so far; it is richer in colour and is clearly far more concerned with recording observed phenomena. Yarmouth Beach was a favourite subject with the Norwich artists, and one which Crome painted on a number of occasions. Such coast scenes were generally popular with British landscapists in this period, and Crome's may be compared with pictures by Turner such as the *Sun Rising through Vapour* (National Gallery) and Joshua Cristall's watercolours of Hastings. In 1822, Constable exhibited a view of Yarmouth Jetty, now in a private collection, which suggests that he may have seen some of Crome's later Yarmouth pictures. Although no Norwich artists are mentioned in Constable's correspondence except the feeble Crome imitator Joseph Paul, it would have been impossible for him to be unaware of their work considering the number of

6. John Crome (1768–1821): *The Beaters*. 1810? Oil on panel, 54 × 85.1 cm. (21¼ × 33½ in.) Edinburgh, National Gallery of Scotland

his friends and acquaintances who visited Norwich or exhibited there.

The influence of Dutch art on Crome's work of this period is seen far more clearly in *Hautbois Common* (Metropolitan Museum, New York) and in *The Beaters* (Plate 6) than in *Yarmouth Jetty*. Although in these glade scenes Crome borrowed Dutch conventions of representing trees and foliage, he invigorated them with his own freedom of handling and created a wonderful illusion of light permeating through leaves and branches. He continued to use paint so thin it revealed the canvas weave, combined with heavy impasto, but the overall effect was now less sketchy. In 1809 the *Norwich Mercury* complained about the presence of 'unfinished' pictures in the exhibition, and it is possible that Crome had found difficulties in selling his early works.

17

By 1810, Ladbrooke too was working in a more solid Dutch-inspired style, as can be seen from his *Mackerel Market on the Beach at Yarmouth* (Plate 8) of that year. It is a picture on a much more ambitious scale than Crome's *Yarmouth Jetty*, but while it is a skilful composition with an admirably planned recession, it lacks the close-knit unity of Crome's picture. Ladbrooke did not share Crome's ability to isolate a pictorial motive in the landscape, or to achieve the delicacy of effect of his *St Martin's Gate* (Plate 9), in which the whole surface seems to glow with light. Precedents for this kind of townscape can again be found in Dutch painting, but *St Martin's Gate* also reflects the contemporary picturesque taste for decaying buildings, a taste which was partly spread through publications such as *Views of Cottages and Farmhouses in England and Wales* (1815) by Francis Stevens, one of Cotman's Sketching Club acquaintances. Stevens exhibited a view of *Carrow Abbey* with the Norwich Society in 1809, and is thus likely to have visited the city. In the years up to 1810, Cotman himself painted a number of dilapidated cottages in various media, an example being the oil sketch illustrated here (Plate 11).

The extent to which Crome's new naturalism was the result of painting in oil out of doors

7. John Crome (1768–1821): *Yarmouth Jetty. c.* 1810.
Oil on canvas, 44.8 × 58.3 cm. (17⅝ × 23 in.) Norwich, Castle Museum

8. Robert Ladbrooke (1769–1842): *Mackerel Market on the Beach at Yarmouth.* Exhibited 1810? Oil on canvas, 84.6 × 142.2 cm. (33¼ × 56 in.) Great Yarmouth Museum

is hard to define. With Constable we can see from a large body of surviving oil sketches how he developed new techniques of representing light and atmosphere outside, even if the technique of most of his finished pictures was ultimately worked out in the studio. Crome, on the other hand, can hardly have been such a prolific sketcher, and few of his oil sketches survive. Two small pictures at Norwich, *Kirkstead Church* and *At Honingham*, could easily have been painted on the spot, and probably date from slightly before *Yarmouth Jetty.* They are far more solidly painted than most outdoor sketches from this period, but they do show a marked

concern with light, and it is possible that studies of this kind did assist Crome to develop more convincing images of the relationship between sky and land. Even so, with two possible exceptions no known Crome oil sketches can be related to finished pictures.

A number of other Norwich artists were producing outdoor oil sketches at this time. Like Crome, Ladbrooke exhibited sketches and studies throughout his career, and his obituarist in the *Art Union Monthly* in 1842 remarked on his 'numerous "sketches" painted entirely on the spot, dispersed by auction shortly after his death, and which, for *simplicity* and *truth*, have very rarely been

19

10. Robert Ladbrooke (1769–1842): *River Yare from Postwick*. After 1820?
Oil on panel, 21.6 × 33 cm. (8½ × 13 in.) Norwich, Castle Museum

surpassed'. In the Castle Museum there is a group of four sketches by Ladbrooke, painted on wooden panels, which certainly help to explain this writer's enthusiasm. The one illustrated here (Plate 10) is lighter in colour and more delicately handled than the others, and is perhaps the latest of the group. Apparently Ladbrooke was particularly preoccupied with sketching after he retired from

9. John Crome (1768–1821): *St Martin's Gate, Norwich*. *c*. 1812–13. Oil on panel, 50.8 × 38 cm. (20 × 15 in.) Norwich, Castle Museum

teaching about 1820, and this sketch may well date from that time. None of these sketches resemble Crome's.

By 1808, Cotman too was making outdoor oil sketches, for one of his exhibits in that year was explicitly described as such in the Norwich Society's catalogue. Even before his return to Norwich, Cotman had been contemplating taking up oil painting, and in 1807 he exhibited a number of portraits, some of which were certainly in oil. His early oils all belong to the years circa 1806–10, after which he seems to have abandoned the medium to concentrate on etching. As well as

portraits, his subjects included classical landscapes, views of old houses, studies of Cromer Beach and seascapes. Although the sketch illustrated in Plate 13 is known as *Duncombe Park*, it appears to be an outdoor sketch, and since Cotman does not seem to have used oil before 1806 it is likely to be a Norfolk view. The subtle effect of light breaking through the trees shows Cotman to have been as capable a sketcher as any Norwich artist, and in these years he quickly achieved mastery of the oil medium. The fresh colouring and bright light effects of sketches such as *Gable End of Old Houses* (Plate 11) and of pictures such as *Old Houses at Gorleston* (Norwich Castle Museum) suggest that they may have helped to bring about Crome's change of style.

Cotman's influence on the Norwich artists is far clearer in the watercolour field. He is not usually thought of as a naturalistic painter, but he was certainly influenced by the naturalist movement among English landscape painters in the period 1800–20. Throughout his life he was a prolific sketcher in pencil and chalk, and between 1800 and 1810 he also made a number of outdoor watercolours. In late 1805 he wrote to Dawson Turner from London describing his activities that summer: 'My chief Study has been colouring from Nature, many of which [studies] are close copies of that fickle Dame, consequently valuable on that account.' This sentence almost certainly refers to the famous drawings he had made in Yorkshire in that year of Duncombe Park, Helmsley Woods, Rokeby Park and Greta Woods. Cotman had been sketching in monochrome out of doors since at least 1800, although he had probably done little sketching in colour. In his finished drawings he had abandoned the dark brown and indigo washes he had employed up to about 1803 (Plate 12) and was using superimposed washes of pure colour in a style related to that of John Varley. It has become

11. John Sell Cotman (1782–1842): *Gable End of Old Houses*. 1806–10. Oil on panel, 42.9 × 33 cm. (16⅞ × 13 in.) Norwich, Castle Museum

12. John Sell Cotman (1782–1842): *Bishops Bridge, Norwich. c.*1802–3.
Watercolour, 21.9 × 33.3 cm. (8⅝ × 13⅛ in.) Norwich, Castle Museum

traditional to emphasize the formal qualities of the Yorkshire drawings, and it has often been said that they were products of the studio. However, while it is true that there are chalk studies for some of the drawings, this does not preclude their being coloured outside. Some of the more elaborate water-colours must have been studio work, but it seems to this author that a number of them, such as *Duncombe Park* (Plate 14), were clearly made on the spot.

Once back in Norwich, Cotman immediately began to play a major role in the city's art life. In the winter of 1806–7 he held a one-man show in his rooms in Wymer Street, and he exhibited a large number of works over the years 1807–12. He was elected to the Norwich Society in 1808, and became Vice-President in 1810 and President in 1811. Among the drawings he exhibited in 1807 were 'A coloured sketch of the Market-place, Norwich, taken from Mr. Cooper's' (Plate 18), and in

23

13 (left). John Sell Cotman (1782–1842): *Duncombe Park*.
1806–10. Oil on canvas, 41.6 × 27.9 cm. (16¾ × 11 in.)
London, Tate Gallery

14 (above). John Sell Cotman (1782–1842): *Duncombe
Park*. 1805. Watercolour, 32.8 × 23 cm. (12⅞ × 9 in.)
London, British Museum

the following year he showed a number of sketches from nature, including three of Yorkshire of which two were made on the spot. After 1808, he does not seem to have exhibited any more sketches of this type, and although some later drawings such as *Bishopgate Bridge* (Plate 16) may have been made outside, generally colouring outdoors was to play a smaller role in his work thereafter.

In the years up to 1810 Cotman's watercolours took on a new strength and intensity of colour, which makes them more strongly illusionistic. *Mousehold Heath* (Plate 17) and *Trowse Hythe* (Plate 19) do not have the same transparency as his earlier drawings, but they would have made more of an impact in exhibition conditions, where they had to hold their own with oil paintings. Some of Cotman's finest renditions of local subjects date from this time, and they show clearly how he was affected by the same poetic ambience as his fellow artists.

If at the time of Cotman's return to Norwich, Crome was the leading exponent of watercolour in the city, it must have been quickly apparent that an artist had now arrived whose talents far exceeded his own. Watercolour was not Crome's main medium of expression, and he never attained the facility of either Cotman or Thirtle. *The Blacksmith's Shop* (Plate 15) probably dates from 1807 or slightly later, and shows that really Crome had taken little advantage of the developments in watercolour technique since Girtin's death. It is a fine composition, but muted in colour and with little atmospheric effect. The colouring and subject of the slightly later *Landscape with Cottages* (Plate 22) also remain essentially picturesque, but this magnificent fluid drawing does suggest that Crome had learnt a new understanding of the possibilities of wash from looking at Cotman's work. None of Crome's finished

15. John Crome (1768–1821): *The Blacksmith's Shop, Hingham.* 1807? Watercolour, 54 × 43.8 cm. (21¼ × 17¼ in.) Norwich, Castle Museum

16. John Sell Cotman (1782–1842): *Bishopsgate Bridge, Norwich. c.*1808–10.
Pencil and watercolour, 25.4 × 45.1 cm. (10 × 17¾ in.) Norwich, Castle Museum

17. John Sell Cotman (1782–1842): *Mousehold Heath. c.*1808–10.
Watercolour, 28.6 × 44.5 cm. (11¼ × 17½ in.) Norwich, Castle Museum

18. John Sell Cotman (1782–1842): *Norwich Market Place*. Exhibited 1807.
Watercolour, 35.6 × 55.9 cm. (14 × 22 in.) Kendal, Abbot Hall Gallery

drawings and very few of his sketches look as if they date from much after 1810, but there is a superb outdoor sketch at Norwich, *Wroxham Regatta*, which is probably the latest watercolour by him to survive. It is more brightly coloured than any of his other drawings, and does suggest that Crome did try to keep up with the developments Thirtle was making in outdoor colouring in the years 1810–20.

It was probably also as a result of Cotman's influence that the watercolours of Robert Dixon and John Thirtle took on a new energy around 1808–10. The most impressive aspect of Dixon's work to survive is a group of outdoor sketches made in Cromer and its neighbourhood, which can be dated to 1809–10 by the Norwich Society catalogues, and by the date on one of them. Dixon's attraction to Cromer was hardly coincidental. It was

19. John Sell Cotman (1782–1842): *Trowse Hythe. c.*1808–10.
Watercolour, 31.8 × 44.1 cm. (12½ × 17⅜ in.) Norwich, Castle Museum

a local beauty spot, celebrated in a poem by Frank Sayers, and when the London artist William Collins visited his friend James Stark in 1815, Stark took him to Cromer where he spent two months making studies of the beach and cliffs. Collins was to exhibit views of Cromer throughout his career, such was the impression the place had made on him.

The Norwich artists may have been encouraged to work at Cromer by a book entitled *Cromer considered as a Watering Place* (1806) by Edmund Bartell, a local surgeon and amateur artist, who became a member of the Norwich Society in 1808, when he exhibited two views of Cromer in the exhibition. His charming and well-written little book is more concerned with the scenery of the place than its facilities, and it shows him thoroughly conversant with the writings of William Gilpin and other picturesque

"Beach Study" RD.

20. Robert Dixon (1780–1815): *Beach Study*. 1809–10.
Watercolour, 8.9 × 21 cm. (3½ × 8¼ in.) Norwich, Castle Museum

theorists. He was particularly enthusiastic about the activities of the fisherfolk on the beach, which were represented by Dixon in a number of drawings (Plate 20), and also about the road to Aylsham (Plate 23).

It is notable that Crome, Cotman and Ladbrooke all exhibited views of Cromer in 1809, and with the exception of Cotman had not done so before, and did not do so again. Cotman had every reason to spend time in Cromer, since Ann Miles, whom he married in January 1809, was the daughter of a farmer at nearby Felbrigg. These coincidences do suggest that the Norwich artists were very aware of each other's work in this period, and if Cotman and Dixon sketched together it would help to explain the new assurance with which the latter began to use coloured wash in his Cromer drawings. Dixon's finished watercolours are few in number, and although they are accomplished works they lack the vitality of his sketches. His early drawings

have some affinities with Crome's, but that illustrated here (Plate 21) shows him trying to achieve the stronger atmospheric effects Thirtle was producing at the same time (Plate 28). Dixon stopped exhibiting in Norwich after 1810, and withdrew from the Society of Artists in 1812, presumably playing a small role in Norwich art in the few remaining years of his life.

Since in 1812 John Thirtle married the sister of Cotman's wife, it is surprising that he exhibited no drawings of Cromer until 1830, and the place hardly features in his firmly attributed works prior to that. According to legend, Thirtle sought out Cotman's drawings in London shop windows when he was training as a frame-maker there in the 1790s, but in fact his early works, particularly some of his monochrome studies, are closer to Crome than to Cotman. Thirtle's exhibits in the years 1806–13 included a substantial number of the river and bridge views at

30

21. Robert Dixon (1780–1815): *St Leonard's Priory, Norwich.* 1809.
Watercolour, 34.6 × 45.4 cm. (13⅝ × 17⅞ in.) Norwich, Castle Museum

which he so excelled. Although Cotman had been making views of the Norwich river as early as 1802–3 (Plate 12), he does not seem to have exhibited any in his first Norwich period, while Crome and Ladbrooke both did. However, Cotman certainly had made the theme of the bridge very much his own, and his work of 1800–6 included views of bridges at York, Knaresborough, Rokeby, Bridgenorth and Durham. The theme was hardly unique to Cotman, who had probably been attracted to it by the example of Girtin, but he did tend to organize his compositions around the central arch of the bridge in a way Girtin had usually not. This type of composition gives Cotman's bridge drawings a balanced quality, which Thirtle emulated (Plate 24).

23. Robert Dixon (1780–1815): *Cromer Road to Aylsham.* 1809–10.
Watercolour, 14.6 × 24.8 cm. (5¾ × 9¾ in.) Norwich, Castle Museum

Thirtle's sketch of the *Devil's Tower* (Plate 27), a view of part of Norwich's medieval defences, is an outdoor study for a drawing which was probably exhibited in 1809 (Plate 28). Together they make an interesting comparison with Crome's sketch of *Houses and Wherries on the Wensum* (Plate 25) and the finished drawing of the same subject in Manchester City Art Gallery. Not only are there similarities in subject-matter, but both artists have relied on the same kind of structure to balance their compositions. How-

22. John Crome (1768–1821): *Landscape with Cottages.*
c. 1808–10. Watercolour, 52.1 × 42.5 cm. (20½ × 16¾ in.)
London, Victoria and Albert Museum

ever, Thirtle's sketch of the *Devil's Tower*, like that of *Whitefriar's Bridge* which is roughly contemporaneous, indicates that he had absorbed more readily than Crome the broader wash technique and richer colouring developed by Cotman and Varley. In the finished drawing (Plate 28), he achieved a stronger illusion of atmospheric effect than Crome ever did in this medium.

Although none of Thirtle's letters has survived, a manuscript treatise on water-colour painting by him has, which confirms that, as with Crome, his overriding concern was with harmony of effect: 'Nature is simple though so unceasingly varied, she is governed by laws & may be read by the Accurate

33

24. John Thirtle (1777–1839): *Whitefriars Bridge, Norwich. c.*1808–10.
Pencil and watercolour, 23.2 × 32.1 cm. (9⅛ × 12⅝ in.) Norwich, Castle Museum

Observor.' This attitude helps to explain his preoccupation with a unified and coherent light effect, with a carefully planned recession, and with the laws of colour harmony. While Thirtle stressed the importance of sketching from nature, he also emphasized that sketches were ultimately fragmentary and incomplete. From at least 1812 onwards, his large watercolours became increasingly finished and detailed, and he began to use stronger colours, perhaps partly influenced by Cotman's drawings of 1808–10. *Boat Builder's Yard near the Cow's Tower* (Plate 26) is probably the drawing of this title exhibited in 1812, and is of particular interest because Crome exhibited a view of the same subject in the following year which would surely have made an interesting comparison with Constable's *Boat-*

25. John Crome (1768–1821): *Houses and Wherries on the Wensum. c.*1808–12.
Watercolour and pencil, 29.8 × 39.7 cm. (11¾ × 15⅝ in.) University of Manchester, Whitworth Art Gallery

Building of 1814 in the Victoria and Albert Museum.

In the period 1810–20 Thirtle's watercolour sketches took on a new facility, as can be seen from *Hoveton Little Broad* (Plate 29). Unlike Cotman, he continued to make out-door watercolours throughout his career, and these were to be an important example to later Norwich artists. However, some of his finished drawings in these years are dis-appointingly artificial compositions, and he often failed to translate the vitality of his sketches onto a larger scale. Thirtle did not exhibit between 1817 and 1828, perhaps partly as a result of his involvement with the Secession, and there are very few finished drawings by him from that time.

One of Thirtle's friends, the Norwich

26. John Thirtle (1777–1839): *Boat-builder's Yard near the Cow's Tower, Norwich.* Exhibited 1812? Water-colour, 44.5 × 65.4 cm. (17½ × 25¾ in.) Norwich, Castle Museum

27. John Thirtle (1777–1839): *Devil's Tower, Norwich*. 1809?
Pencil and watercolour, 23 × 30.2 cm. (9 × 11⅞ in.) Norwich, Castle Museum

portraitist Joseph Clover (1779–1853), also achieved an extraordinarily high standard in a group of watercolour sketches of 1810. Clover began his career as an engraver and was encouraged to take up painting by Opie. Although he was resident in London by 1804 he made repeated visits to Norwich, painting the civic dignitaries and other local worthies, and often exhibiting there. He was a friend of Thomas Harvey and probably a familiar of both Crome and Cotman. Most of the watercolours by him in the Norwich Castle Museum seem to date from a trip to Northumberland and Durham in 1810, but at least one is a Norfolk view, and he clearly made other sketches in the county. Drawings such as

38

28. John Thirtle (1777–1839): *Devil's Tower near King Street Gates, Evening*. Exhibited 1809?
Pencil, watercolour and white bodycolour, 33.3 × 43.8 cm. (13⅛ × 17¼ in.) Norwich, Castle Museum

In Chipchase Park (Plate 30), with their wonderful spontaneous technique and strong sense of design, were probably only occasional productions, since Clover was not primarily a landscapist, but they do suggest his involvement with the other Norwich artists.

It is impossible to prove that Cotman's arrival in Norwich inspired the burgeoning of watercolour among the Norwich artists around 1808–10. The work of John Varley, De Wint and Cristall could easily be seen in the London exhibitions, and Varley actually exhibited in Norwich in 1809. But Cotman was a far greater artist than any of these, and he does seem the obvious catalyst.

*

39

29. John Thirtle (1777–1839) *Hoveton Little Broad. c.* 1815–20.
Watercolour, 22.5 × 32.7 cm. (8⅞ × 12⅞ in.) Norwich, Castle Museum

The idea of mutual influences among the Norwich artists is further confirmed by the spate of etchings they began to produce about 1809. In the early twentieth century, Crome's etchings were widely admired because, like some of those later produced by Andrew Geddes, they seemed to use etching as a sketching medium rather than as a reproductive one. Unfortunately, many of Crome's etchings were finished by later hands and they can only be appreciated in their early states. Although he issued a prospectus in 1812, Crome himself seems to have regarded the prints as unfinished too, and they were only published after his death.

It is uncertain which of the Norwich artists first took up etching, but it may have been the amateur Thomas Harvey, who produced a number of soft-ground etchings probably inspired by those of Gainsborough. The Norwich-born musical prodigy, Dr William Crotch, was certainly making soft-ground etchings by 1809, and a group of these were in a sale of prints, paintings and drawings which Crome held in Yarmouth in 1812. In any case soft-ground etching was something of a

30. Joseph Clover (1779–1853): *In Chipchase Park*. 1810.
Watercolour, 25.4 × 18.1 cm. (10 × 7⅛ in.) Norwich, Castle Museum

fashion in the first decade of the century. Crotch's friend William Delamotte had published his *Forest Trees* in 1804, and in 1810 Cotman's friend Louis Francia published a series of soft-ground prints after Gainsborough, Girtin, Varley and others. Francia also visited Norwich about this time.

Thirty-three of Crome's etchings survive, and of these nine are dated variously between 1809 and 1813. Robert Dixon was working on his etchings of *Picturesque Scenery of Norfolk* by 1810, although their publication date is 1811, and the earliest of the series of etchings Cotman published in that year is also dated 1810. It is probable that Crome's earliest prints were his nine soft-ground plates (Plate 31), since this technique did not involve re-biting and was easier to master. Its effect is like that of a soft-pencil drawing, and basically the process reproduces a pencil drawing. Crome's hard-ground plates caused him far more problems, and in these he looked clearly to the example of the seventeenth-century Dutch masters, particularly Ruisdael. Dixon was a far less proficient craftsman than Crome and all of his plates were in soft-ground with two exceptions. The *Sketch on Cromer Beach* (Plate 32) illustrated here makes an interesting comparison in subject and composition with Crome's *Yarmouth Jetty* (Plate 7). Most of Dixon's etchings were of picturesque cottages, and not of simple bits of scenery like Crome's.

Cotman, too, made soft-ground etchings, but mainly in the years 1814–17, when ill-health probably encouraged him to investigate the easier process. His main output as a printmaker was of a different order from that of Crome and Dixon, and of the Norwich artists he alone made prints a major source of income for a period of his life. Crome and Dixon made their prints either for amusement or for amateur pupils to copy. Although the 24 plates of Cotman's first publication were miscellaneous in subject, they were predominantly architectural, and he had already decided to model himself on the great Italian etcher Piranesi. In 1811 he began work on a series of 60 etchings, *The Architectural Antiquities of Norfolk*, which was not completed until 1818, and was intended to illustrate Blomefield's monumental history of the county. In the same period he also produced more than 100 other prints of local antiquities, and more than 150 etchings of East Anglian church brasses. All this activity culminated in his most ambitious publication, *The Architectural Antiquities of Normandy*, 97 plates made over the years 1818–21, which involved him in three trips to France. His preoccupation with etching meant that he largely abandoned painting in both watercolour and oil over the years 1810–21.

In April 1812 Cotman moved to Yarmouth to take up the salary of £200 a year which Dawson Turner had offered him to teach drawing to his family, and he did not return to Norwich until December 1823. Turner wrote the text to the *Antiquities of Normandy*, and he undoubtedly encouraged Cotman to concentrate on his architectural prints. Such prints are not what modern critics regard as 'original etchings', and about late 1813 he began to employ assistants to undertake less important prints and the routine parts of the process. Although his ambition was to become an English Piranesi, and some of his early plates were influenced by Piranesi in conception and technique (Plate 33), his publications were really closer to those of his friend the

31 (opposite above). John Crome (1768–1821): *At Bixley. c.* 1809. Soft-ground etching, 16.5 × 23.7 cm. (6½ × 9¼ in.) London, British Museum

32 (opposite below). Robert Dixon (1780–1815): *Sketch on Cromer Beach.* 1810–11. Soft-ground etching, 20 × 24.9 cm. (7⅞ × 9¾ in.) Norwich, Castle Museum

42

Rob.t Dixon fec.t   Sketch on Cromer Beach

33. John Sell Cotman (1782–1842): *Castle Rising Castle*. 24.1 × 36.8 cm. (9½ × 14½ in.) Plate xxvi from Cotman's *A Series of Etchings Illustrative of the Architectural Antiquities of Norfolk*, London, 1818. Photo: British Library

English antiquarian publicist John Britton. In Cotman's day the distinction between engraving and etching was not clearly defined, and while he sought to give a new vitality to the architectural print, he increasingly based his style on that of contemporary engravers such as George Cooke and Henry Le Keux. Although in the nineteenth century his reputation as a printmaker was very high, he has hardly received the recognition he deserves since.

A number of other Norwich artists including Robert Ladbrooke, James Sillett and Henry Ninham also produced publications of archi-tectural antiquities, which were either etched or lithographed. Unlike theirs, however, Cotman's publications were not just directed at a local market, and his ultimate failure to earn by them the rewards and reputation he craved for led to a breakdown in his health. With Crome dead, he returned to Norwich where he established a new ascendancy in the city's art life.

*

34. John Crome (1768–1821): *Postwick Grove*. c. 1814–17. Oil on millboard, 48.9 × 40.6 cm. (19¼ × 16 in.) Norwich, Castle Museum

35. Joseph Clover (1779–1853): *Whitlingham Church, near Norwich*. 1822.
Oil on millboard, 35.6 × 27.9 cm. (14 × 11 in.) Norwich, Castle Museum

At the time Cotman had left Norwich, Crome was either the leading artist in the city or was fast becoming so, and his position was to be strengthened both by the increasing sophistication of his work, and by the coming to maturity of his three most talented pupils. In 1814, Crome, like many other British artists, visited Paris to see the treasures of the Musée Napoleon, travelling in company with a Norwich amateur, Daniel Coppin, and the dealer William Freeman. Crome did the usual things: he studied in the Louvre, visited the studios of David and other French artists, and bought materials at the celebrated colour shops. He also exhibited in a Paris exhibition and bought a number of pictures which he smuggled past the customs. Perhaps like Andrew Robertson he called on the French landscapist Bidault and saw his oil sketches and pictures painted on the spot, but his opinion of French art in general was low.

The experience inspired at least three of his major paintings, one of which, the *Boulevard des Italiens* (Collection of R. Q. Gurney Esq.), is a view of a Paris street scene which he exhibited in 1815. It is one of the first paintings to reflect the craze for representations of continental scenery to which the British public succumbed after 1814. Stylistically the *Boulevard des Italiens* relates to the Lever Art Gallery's *Marlingford Grove* and the Castle Museum's sketch of *Postwick Grove* (Plate

34). In these pictures the tree structure is not defined so much in terms of separate branches as it had been in say *The Beaters*, but as touches of light green paint laid over those of a darker hue, which broadly suggest the effect of light on foliage. Their colouring is also brighter, and they have a more naturalistic atmosphere than anything he had painted previously. *Postwick Grove* suggests that the new style was partly developed outdoors, and this new sophistication in outdoor oil painting in Norwich is probably also reflected in a number of sketches by Joseph Clover such as *Whitlingham Church* (Plate 35) of 1822.

Crome's new command of light and colour can be seen in *The Poringland Oak* (frontispiece), which has traditionally been connected with a picture of 1818 shown at the 1821 Memorial Exhibition. In its close-knit composition *Poringland Oak* resembles some of Crome's etchings, and the clearly articulated tree structure looks back to pictures like *The Beaters*. However, by 1819 his style had undergone a final transformation. In that year, the reviewer in the *Norfolk Chronicle*, who in 1815 had described *Boulevard des Italiens* as a 'spirited sketch', complained that several of his pictures should more properly be called studies, and the *Norwich Mercury* noted one picture 'in a new manner', 'light and airy in its execution, and very clear in its particular parts'. The Norwich artist David Hodgson, writing in the 1850s, described Crome's last works as 'combining at once the plastic coloring of Ruysdael with the grace and light handling of Gainsborough'.

Such a description seems to fit perfectly *The Willow Tree* (Plate 37), a finished picture which has a freedom of handling comparable with Corot's work. The superb airy effect of this painting resembles that of *The Fishmarket, Boulogne* (Plate 38), exhibited in 1820, which the *Norfolk Chronicle* again criticized for its lack of finish. In these last pictures Crome seems to have been moving away from the tight architectonic structures of his earlier works towards more casual compositions, but his sudden and tragic death in 1821 cut short this development towards new heights of atmospheric naturalism.

By contrast, Robert Ladbrooke, who lived on until 1842, responded less readily to the general trends in English landscape painting in the years 1810–20. *Foundry Bridge* (Plate 39) was probably a later variant of a picture exhibited with the Norwich Society in 1815, but there seems little to distinguish the style of this from the works of 1810, and it is equally dark and solid in execution. To judge from photographs, *Merry Making, with a View of Norwich, from Richmond Hill Gardens* (private collection), exhibited in the following year, is similar in quality. While none of Ladbrooke's pastiches of the old masters has been identified, a number of pictures comparable in subject to Crome's are recorded in photographs and prints, and there is also a *Wroxham Water Frolic* (private collection) which makes an interesting comparison with John Berney Crome's *Yarmouth Water Frolic* (Plate 40). Ladbrooke's *Landscape with Pigs* (Plate 36) cannot be dated, but its brighter colouring and broader handling suggest that it is later than any of the works discussed so far. With the collapse of the Secession exhibitions after 1818 Ladbrooke ceased to exhibit in Norwich until 1824, although he showed four pictures in London during these years. Ladbrooke exhibited occasionally in Norwich between 1824 and 1837, but he seems to have retired about 1822, when he handed over his teaching practice to his sons. In 1821 he began making drawings of the Norwich churches, which were the basis for the 677 lithographs finally published by his son John Berney in 1843. His other main hobby seems to have been making outdoor sketches, but he certainly continued to produce finished pictures too.

36. Robert Ladbrooke (1769–1842): *Landscape with Pigs*. After 1820. Oil on canvas, 64.8 × 76.2 cm. (25½ × 30 in.)
Private collection

The Norwich Society could hardly have withstood the secession of some of its most consistent exhibitors had not three of Crome's pupils, all in their early twenties, been able to make a substantial showing. We know from various accounts which have come down to us and from the evidence of pupils' drawings that Crome taught amateurs how to draw from nature, although they also made copies after his works which they sometimes exhibited. His professional pupils seem to have had a similar type of instruction, and while both Stark and Vincent made copies in their early years they ultimately developed styles quite distinct from that of their master.

Not surprisingly, his son John Berney (1794–1842) was Crome's most precocious follower. A successful pupil at the Norwich

37. John Crome (1768–1821): *The Willow Tree*. 1820–21.
Oil on canvas, 128.9 × 103.8 cm. (50¾ × 40⅞ in.) Nottingham, Castle Museum

Grammar School, at twelve he was already painting in oil, by sixteen he was sketching in watercolour on the spot, and at seventeen he was exhibiting pictures for sale. In 1819 he was president of the Norwich Society. He seems to have inherited the personal charm of his father, he was articulate and a good public speaker, and he is said to have attained 'considerable classical acquirement'. On his father's death he took over the teaching practice and became probably the leading figure in the Norwich art world. The *Norwich Mercury*, reviewing one of his pictures in 1822, felt that he promised 'to surpass the talents of his father'. Unfortunately this promise was never fulfilled.

Although J. B. Crome's work was generally well received in Norwich, London and other cities, by 1866 his reputation had fallen to the extent that the brothers Redgrave did not even mention him in their *Century of Painters*. The work of his co-pupils Stark and Vincent was highly sought after by the end of the century, but J. B. Crome hardly features in Graves's *Art Sales* (1918–21). However, if he was a less individual talent than they were, he should not just be known by the interminable moonlight scenes which dominated his production from the mid-1820s onwards.

In the years 1814–18 J. B. Crome exhibited a large number of oil sketches, some of them explicitly described as 'painted on the spot', and some of which were studies for larger pictures. He had certainly exhibited watercolours produced in this way before and perhaps oils too, but thereafter he was to show fewer sketches, and this is a pattern we can see with other Norwich artists. Quite a number of his broadly painted sketches of moonlight effects survive, and there are examples in the Norwich Castle Museum, the Victoria and Albert Museum and the Tate Gallery. He was a less distinguished draughtsman than his father, and in 1812 he began exhibiting sketches in black and white chalk, a technique he favoured throughout his career, and which perhaps encouraged the slick and facile execution of his oils.

The extremely high standard of which J. B. Crome was sometimes capable is clearly illustrated by *Yarmouth Water Frolic* (Plates 40 and 41), which is based on a sketch by his father, and which was possibly begun by him. J. B. Crome added more details to his father's design, and the picture has a more laboured surface than most of Crome's. *Yarmouth Water Frolic* has often been compared with Turner's *The Dort Packet-Boat from Rotterdam Becalmed* of 1818 (Paul Mellon Collection), and Turner was to be a continuing influence on J. B. Crome's work. It should equally be noted that in 1819 Stark had exhibited a large picture of a sailing match at Wroxham at the British Institution, and this precedent may also have been in Crome's mind.

While he never lived outside Norfolk, J. B. Crome did travel in Holland and France and exhibited a large number of pictures of continental scenery. In this he was following a trend of the time, but it does mean that the local associations which suffused his father's works were to some extent lost in his. He visited France for the first time in 1816, and from 1817 he exhibited a number of views of Rouen, some of them based on oil sketches he had made on the spot. The example illustrated here (Plate 42) was probably one of those exhibited in 1822 or 1823, and it already suggests that without his father to guide him

38 (opposite above). John Crome (1768–1821): *The Fishmarket, Boulogne*. Exhibited 1820. Oil on canvas, 52.7 × 86 cm. (20¾ × 33⅞ in.) Norwich, Castle Museum

39 (opposite below). Robert Ladbrooke (1769–1842): *Foundry Bridge, Norwich*. After 1815. Oil on canvas, 66.7 × 98.4 cm. (26¼ × 38¾ in.) Norwich, Castle Museum

40 and 41 (detail). John Berney Crome (1794–1842): *Yarmouth Water Frolic—Evening; Boats Assembling previous to the Rowing Match*. Exhibited 1821. Oil on canvas, 106 × 172.7 cm. (41¾ × 68 in.) Greater London Council as Trustees of the Iveagh Bequest, Kenwood

he could not sustain the high quality of *Yarmouth Water Frolic*.

In their *Dictionary of Artists of the English School* (1878) the Redgraves said of J. B. Crome: 'His works were very unequal and he never took any place in art.' Indeed, some of his pictures are embarrassingly bad, but even as late as 1832 he could produce works such as *Near Bury St Edmunds* (Plate 44), which despite its rather synthetic colouring is a well-planned composition painted in a broad style somewhat reminiscent of his father's late work. With Crome one is dealing with a highly intelligent artist, whose work reflects a continuing assimilation of old and modern masters, combined with new techniques evolved to express his own perceptions. With J. B. Crome there seems no intelligent pattern of development.

J. B. Crome went bankrupt in 1834 and moved to Yarmouth where he remained until his death, plagued by health problems and perhaps drink problems too. He had played a very active role in the Norwich Society, and whatever his calibre as an artist, his departure must have contributed considerably to its collapse.

In 1831, the *Norwich Mercury*, reviewing two pictures by James Stark, remarked:

There is no specimen of the true Norwich School—that founded by the deceased Mr. Crome—so perfect in its peculiar distinctions, for no artist preserves the principle while he advances and elevates the practice as much as Mr. Stark.

Stark was born in Norwich in 1794, the son of a Scottish dyer, a man of considerable scientific and literary culture. He was fellow pupil of J. B. Crome at the Norwich Grammar

52

School, and in 1811 he was articled to Crome senior for three years. Soon after his articles expired, Stark moved to London where he entered the Academy Schools in 1817. He became a friend of the painter William Collins, who knew both Linnell and Constable, and under whose influence he seems to have fallen.

Although he began exhibiting in London in 1811, Stark's first major success seems to have come in 1815, when the Dean of Windsor bought his picture *The Bathing Place— Morning* at the British Institution exhibition. In 1818, his *Penning the Flock* was bought from the same gallery by the Marquis of Stafford and he sold two other works to aristocratic patrons. He subsequently sold pictures to the academicians Chantrey, Phillips and Sir George Beaumont. It must have seemed that he was likely to earn a far wider reputation than Crome ever had, until in 1819 ill health forced him to return to Norwich, where he remained until 1830.

One of Stark's early pictures, *Lambeth, looking towards Westminster Bridge*, bought by the Countess de Grey from the British Institution in 1818, is now in the Paul Mellon Collection. It shows that to begin with Stark worked in a fairly broad naturalistic style comparable with that of his fellow pupils. None of Stark's exhibited works are explicitly described as outdoor oil sketches, but a number by him are known, and he was also a prolific sketcher in chalk and water-colours. The beautiful sketch shown in Plate 43 is related to the picture of the same title exhibited in 1818. Despite its outdoor quality it shows the preoccupation with detail which is a feature of much of Stark's work, and it is

42. John Berney Crome (1794–1842): *Rouen*. 1822–3? Oil on canvas, 74 × 102.2 cm. (29⅛ × 40¼ in.) Norwich, Castle Museum

43. James Stark (1794–1859): *Penning the Flock. c.*1818.
Oil on panel, 22.9 × 27.9 cm. (9 × 11 in.) Norwich, Castle Museum

certainly significant that in his letter of 1816 Crome had particularly recommended him to consider 'breadth'. To judge from its colouring and technique, *Whitlingham* (Plate 45) probably dates from the early 1840s. Although it could be regarded as a finished picture, it too has the appearance of having been painted on the spot.

Stark's early paintings are so rich in natural effect that it is hard to understand the repetitive stylized quality of some of his later landscapes, unless like J. B. Crome he found a good selling line. Unfortunately, he has become best known for his numerous glade scenes in imitation of Hobbema, following a pattern which Crome had set with *Hautbois Common*. But whereas Crome had invigorated the Hobbema formula with a new richness of effect, Stark became a pasticheur. His trees look

44. John Berney Crome (1794–1842): *Near Bury St Edmunds.* 1832. Oil on canvas, 113 × 94 cm. (44½ × 37 in.) Norwich, Castle Museum

56

45. James Stark (1794–1859): *Whitlingham*. Early 1840s?
Oil on canvas, 42.5 × 60.3 cm. (16¾ × 23¾ in.) Norwich, Castle Museum

like broccoli (Plate 47), and their colouring is synthetic and predictable, each picture containing a contrast of ochre, red and green. In September 1825, the *London Magazine*, which had been enthusiastic about Stark's work in the early 1820s, commented: '. . . we must object to his iteration of subject; a practise which shows that he is more conversant with Hobbema and Ruysdael than with nature. . . . If there is but one subject, there is also but one system of colour and of management. . . . What he has done is good; but he has as yet painted but one picture.' To judge from exhibition catalogues, Stark produced most of these pastiches in the 1820s,

when he exhibited a number of works simply called 'Landscape'. Thereafter most of his exhibits have topographical titles.

In 1827, Stark began work on a very ambitious undertaking, which although well received was not a financial success. This was a series of pictures, recording local scenery then undergoing changes as a result of improvements in river navigation between Norwich and the coast, which were the basis for a book of 35 engravings, *The Rivers of Norfolk*. This followed the pattern of earlier topographical publications such as the Cookes' *Southern Coast*, and indeed the Cookes engraved some of Stark's plates. Although

58

46. James Stark (1794–1859): *Postwick Grove*. 11.8 × 16.8 cm. (4⅝ × 6⅝ in.) Engraving from J. W. Robberds, *Scenery of the Rivers of Norfolk, from Pictures painted by James Stark*, Norwich and London, 1834. Photo: Norwich Castle Museum

a number of the engravings are of Hobbema-like scenes (Plate 46), Stark was obviously forced to pay real attention to topography. *View on the Yare near Thorpe Church* (Plate 50) records a local holiday spot, a favourite subject with Norwich artists. Its strong natural light effect and brighter colour range show Stark clearly moving away from the formulas of the glade scenes.

The Norwich newspaper reviews and Norwich Society catalogues suggest that Stark continued to exhibit his pastiches as late as 1832, but in 1829 the critic in the *Norfolk Chronicle*, who tended to favour painting manifestly indebted to the old masters, com-plained of a new style visible in Stark's beach scenes, which were 'hard in manner and surcharged with colour'. In 1839, the *Norwich Mercury* commented generally that his land-scapes were 'brilliant with beauty and light. The exchange from Hobbima to nature is indeed a marvellous improvement.' Perhaps partly owing to the influence of Joseph Stannard (Plate 59), Stark had developed a style better suited to the London exhi-bitions at which he had begun to show an increasing number of works, and where landscapes were in a brighter key of colouring then ever before. In 1830 he returned to London, where he seems to have been

47. James Stark (1794–1859): *Wooded Landscape. c.*1822–32.
Oil on panel, 32.4 × 42.5 cm. (13¾ × 16¾ in.) Port Sunlight, Wirral, Lady Lever Collection

reasonably successful. The painting of *Cromer* illustrated here (Plate 48) was probably that exhibited at the British Institution in 1837, and it clearly reveals the influence of his friend William Collins. Like a number of others, this picture is based on an outdoor watercolour and chalk study, and Stark's vast output of sketches of this type (Plate 49) helps to explain the new freshness of some of his later paintings. It is quite likely that his use of the outdoor watercolour was inspired by the example of Thirtle (Plate 29).

In 1840 Stark moved to Windsor, where he made many paintings of the forest, which show a far sounder grasp of tree structure than his earlier glade scenes (Plate 51). He never lived in Norwich again, he exhibited fewer pictures of Norfolk subjects, and his later style had little to connect it with the Norwich School. Stark had a number of pupils, including Samuel Colkett, Alfred Priest and his son Arthur James Stark, none of whom was significant. Many pathetically bad works attributed to Stark cannot be by him.

60

48. James Stark (1794–1859): *Cromer*. Exhibited 1837?
Oil on panel, 60.6 × 85.7 cm. (23⅞ × 33¾ in.) Norwich, Castle Museum

Although in 1831 the *Norwich Mercury* described Stark as Crome's closest follower, to many later commentators George Vincent has seemed the true continuator of Crome's principles. Vincent, who was to die in the following year, had seldom visited Norwich in the 1820s, his moral reputation there being under a cloud, and this may partly be why the *Mercury* chose to see Stark as Crome's heir. Born in 1796, like Stark he became a friend of J. B. Crome while at the Grammar School, and was later apprenticed to his father. In 1816

Vincent accompanied J. B. Crome on a trip to Paris, apparently suffering much discomfiture from 'belshing' on the crossing. A painting by him of *Rouen in 1816* (Norwich Castle Museum) was probably painted shortly after, and may have been inspired by Crome's *Boulevard des Italiens*. It is just as broadly painted as Crome's work at that time, but it is marred by inconsistencies of scale and perspective, an aspect of his art which Vincent never quite mastered.

61

Vincent does not seem to have moved to London until 1818, and although he may have lived in the same house as Stark, he did not enter the Academy Schools. In 1819 the *Norwich Mercury* remarked on his success in the metropolis, and in 1820 he sold a large view of *London from Waterloo Bridge* to the important patron Sir John Leicester. To judge from an etching of it, this was a self-consciously Claudean picture in some ways resembling Turner's Claudean sea ports. One of the pictures Vincent exhibited in Norwich in 1820, *Sheep Crossing a Brook* (Plate 54), can be identified from a long and enthusiastic description in the *Norfolk Chronicle*. It is a freshly coloured picture with a less clearly ordered composition than most of Crome's, and it already shows Vincent as a distinctive and original artist.

In 1821 Thomas Griffiths Wainwright, reviewing the exhibition at the British Institution in the *London Magazine*, singled out for special praise Crome's *Heath Scene near Norwich* and Vincent's *Dutch Fair on Yarmouth Beach* (Plate 55). Cotman had exhibited an unfinished drawing of the Dutch Fair in Norwich in 1809, but Vincent was probably more conscious of the precedent of Crome's *Fishmarket, Boulogne* (Plate 38). Vincent's work tends to be on a much more ambitious scale than Crome's, and it is often more Turnerian in its expansive compositions and profusion of incident. Although this type of beach subject can be traced back to the Dutch School, Vincent's picture is far closer in conception to Turner's *St Mawes at the*

49 (opposite above). James Stark (1794–1859): *Sand Dunes, Caister. c.* 1835. Pencil and watercolour, 24.8 × 33 cm. (9¾ × 13 in.) Norwich, Castle Museum

50 (opposite below). James Stark (1794–1859): *View on the Yare near Thorpe Church. c.* 1825-8. Oil on panel, 42.5 × 55.9 cm. (16¾ × 22 in.) Norwich, Castle Museum

51. James Stark (1794–1859): *Distant View of Windsor.* 1840s? Oil on panel, 26.7 × 21.3 cm. (10½ × 8⅜ in.) London, Victoria and Albert Museum

Pilchard Season (Tate Gallery, exhibited in 1812) than to any seventeenth-century picture.

Like Crome, Vincent was repeatedly attracted to the subject of Yarmouth beach, and he painted several variants on the theme of the fish market, two of which, dated 1827 and 1828, are in the Norwich Castle Museum. Again, they are larger and more profuse than Crome's Yarmouth Beach paintings, and that of 1827 invites comparison with Constable's *Chain Pier, Brighton* (Tate Gallery, exhibited in 1827). Pictures like these help to explain why the Redgraves in their *Century of Painters* suggested that of Constable's contemporaries and successors, only Vincent had made the same 'treatment of his subject'. By which they meant: 'the thorough abstraction of . . . attention from details, to concentrate his whole feeling on the general effects of nature', or 'breadth'. Perhaps they had forgotten about Turner.

Vincent's work was not, however, founded on the same principles of disciplined study as Constable's, and few of his drawings and sketches have survived. Certain features of his landscapes became rather stereotyped, particularly his handling of foliage, and the magnificent cloud formations with which, like Constable, he balanced his compositions. As with Stark, none of his exhibits were explicitly described as oil sketches painted on the spot, but a few small pictures such as that illustrated in Plate 53 at least have the appearance of outdoor work. He did not have the same intellectual and moral drive as Constable, and after he got into financial difficulties some of his output fell off disastrously in quality, a decline noted by the *Norwich Mercury* in 1825.

By April 1821 Vincent was apparently in 'very indifferent health', although he managed to return to Norwich for Crome's funeral in that month. His marriage in 1822 does not seem to have come at a very auspicious moment, for at some point in that year he was obliged 'to sell everything off', and he is said to have married for money but been disappointed. Most of our information about Vincent's subsequent career comes from an extremely interesting series of letters written by him to William Davey, one of Stark's neighbours in Norwich, over the years 1824–7. These reveal that Vincent had been guilty of some 'past folly', which had brought him into debt, and led to a breach of his relations both with his parents and with Stark. Through Davey, he attempted to sell a number of pictures in Norwich for very low prices, and in December 1824 he was confined to the Fleet Prison for debt, not obtaining his release until early in 1827.

Considering the circumstances of his later years, Vincent still produced some fine pictures, but he probably never painted anything quite so ambitious as the *Distant View of Pevensey Bay, the Landing Place of King William the Conqueror* (Plate 52), which he exhibited at the British Institution in 1824, and which received very favourable reviews in the London papers. Its bright colouring and manificent panoramic space again show Vincent emulating Turner, and like so many of Turner's subjects, the view had associations with a great historical event. Although he continued to exhibit Norfolk views, Vincent restricted himself less to local subject-matter in the 1820s, and in this his development resembles that of other Norwich artists. In 1819 he visited Scotland, and from 1820 onwards exhibited a number of Scottish scenes,

52 (opposite above). George Vincent (1796–1832): *View of Beachy Head from Pevensey*. Exhibited in 1824 as *Distant View of Pevensey Bay, the Landing Place of King William the Conqueror*. Oil on canvas, 146.1 × 233.6 cm. (57½ × 92 in.) Norwich, Castle Museum

53 (opposite below). George Vincent (1796–1832): *Wooded Landscape with Figures and Gate*. 1820s? Oil on panel, 27.6 × 35.6 cm. (10⅞ × 14 in.) City of Manchester Art Galleries

54. George Vincent (1796–1832): *Driving the Flock, St Mary's, Beverley*. Exhibited in 1820 as *Sheep Crossing a Brook*. Oil on canvas, 101.6 × 127 cm. (40 × 50 in.) Private collection

several of which still survive. Perhaps the most romantic of these is the striking moonlight view, *Loch Katrine—Highlanders Spearing Salmon* (Norwich Castle Museum), which was exhibited in Norwich in 1825 and at the British Institution in the following year.

Unlike his master and fellow pupils, Vincent regularly signed and dated his work, and many pictures by him are dated in the late 1820s. *Trowse Meadows* (Plate 57), although it is not dated, is usually associated with a picture exhibited in 1828, and is one of the most impressive of his late works. It inevitably invites comparison with Constable's *Haywain* (exhibited in 1821), and while it obviously has a more Claudean structure than that

picture, it still preserves a sense of place. The handling of *Trowse Meadows* does not have the transparency and glitter of Constable's paintwork, but the perspective of the clouds, the light effect and the atmospheric recession are all superbly suggested. Vincent was an uneven artist, but he was certainly as capable as many of his better-known contemporaries.

*

Although two of Ladbrooke's sons, Henry (1800–69) and John Berney (1803–79), are said to have studied with Crome, if they did the experience left no discernible effect on their work, and they probably learnt most from their father. Both of them remained

66

55. George Vincent (1796–1832): *Dutch Fair on Yarmouth Beach*. Exhibited 1821.
Oil on canvas, 112.2 × 143.5 cm. (44⅛ × 56½ in.) Great Yarmouth Museum

essentially local artists, who earned a living by teaching drawing. John Berney Ladbrooke was the more significant artist, partly because his output was so large, but also because of his influence on a number of other painters, the most gifted of whom was John Middleton. His typical subjects are grove scenes of a type comparable to those of Stark and Vincent, but he also painted views of Scotland and the Lake District. He worked in a rather harsh colour range with a finicky touch, and his pictures have the cloying prettiness and repetitive execution of Victorian landscapes by artists such as Thomas Creswick and Frederick Lee. Henry Ladbrooke complained in his manuscript reminiscences that his father's training had involved more copying than studying from nature, and this seems verified by his own and his brother's work. John Berney Ladbrooke did play some role in the Norwich Society from 1828 onwards, although he was never one of its officers.

Ladbrooke's most gifted pupil was Joseph Stannard (1797–1830), and after Crome and Cotman he was probably the most distinguished painter to work in Norwich. He received little notice either in nineteenth-century accounts of the Norwich School, or in histories and dictionaries of British painting, perhaps because his career was so short, and also because he never lived outside Norwich for any period of time. His work seems to have

67

56. Joseph Stannard (1797–1830): *Thorpe Water Frolic—Afternoon.* Exhibited 1825.
Oil on canvas, 108 × 172.7 cm. (42½ × 68 in.) Norwich, Castle Museum

been very popular with local collectors, but he exhibited in Norwich irregularly and in some years showed only in London. Since he suffered from ill health and his output was not very large, he may have had nothing left to show after selling his works in the London exhibitions, which preceded those in Norwich. Stannard followed Ladbrooke in the 1816 Secession and he never became a member of the Norwich Society. Like Ladbrooke, he exhibited a large number of pictures simply called 'Landscape' or 'Landscape Composition' in the years 1817–18, which suggests that he too was producing pastiches of the old masters at this time. It was not until the early 1820s that he began to receive any attention in the Norwich press.

In 1821 Stannard visited Holland to study the picture collections there, and in the following year he exhibited a copy after Berchem's *The Ferry* in the Rijksmuseum. His choice of Berchem is significant, because his own work often has the rather hard bright colouring and brilliant light effects of that master. Stannard's style has no real affinities with that of Crome and his pupils, and his work tended to be highly finished like that of the Dutch masters. Some of his sea pieces are transparently inspired by the Van de Veldes. However, Stannard was not just a pasticheur, and he achieved more natural illusions of light and atmospheric effect than they usually had, and painted in a far brighter range of colours (Plate 58). In this combination of qualities, his works are sometimes reminiscent of pictures by John Linnell and William Mulready from 1811–13, and he may have had some contact with Linnell, who knew his friend E. T. Daniell at least by 1822.

In his choice of subjects, Stannard was very much a member of the Norwich School, and nearly all his views were of local scenes. He owned a number of pictures by Crome, and a small view of the river at Thorpe by him in the Castle Museum was possibly inspired by Crome's painting of a similar view made about 1806. Equally, his views of Yarmouth beach invite comparison with those of Crome, Ladbrooke and Vincent. The example illustrated here (Plate 59) was possibly a picture exhibited in Norwich in 1829. Stannard's work on a large scale was naturally more broadly painted than small pictures like this, but it shows the same fascination with natural detail. His masterpiece, *Thorpe Water Frolic* (Plate 56), continues the tradition of holiday subjects to which J. B. Crome's *Yar-*

mouth Water Frolic (Plate 40) also belongs. The effect of light and atmosphere in this picture was beyond the range of any other Norwich artist at this time except Vincent, whose influence might be seen in the cloud formation. It is a picture which clearly illustrates the fusion of poetry and truth in Norwich painting, a combination upon which the *Norwich Mercury* commented when it was exhibited in 1825. The event depicted was one of a series of water frolics organized by John Harvey of Thorpe Lodge, but the brilliant atmosphere and scale of the event suggest a certain amount of poetic licence. The *Norwich Mercury* commented on the strong blues in the picture, which can also be found in the large *River Yare at Thorpe* in the Castle Museum, and this use of blue to suggest the colour of sunlight may mean that Stannard had been affected by reading Henry Richter's *Daylight, A Recent Discovery in the Art of Painting* (1817), or by the strong blues Cotman employed in his drawings of the 1820s

57. George Vincent (1796–1832): *Trowse Meadows, near Norwich*. Exhibited 1828?
Oil on canvas, 73 × 109.5 cm. (28¾ × 43⅛ in.) Norwich, Castle Museum

58. Joseph Stannard (1797–1830): *Buckenham Ferry*. 1826.
Oil on panel, 40 × 61 cm. (15¾ × 24 in.) New Haven, Connecticut, Yale Center for British Art, Paul Mellon Collection

The question arises again with Stannard of how far the naturalistic elements in his style were the result of outdoor painting. None of his exhibited works were explicitly described as 'painted on the spot', but he certainly made watercolour sketches from nature, which were later used as the basis for oil paintings, such as the drawing of *Buckenham Ferry* illustrated here (cf Plates 58 and 62). He also made many fine studies in coloured chalk. In 1828, Stannard's brother Alfred exhibited quite a large picture of Trowse Hall at the British Institution, which was described as painted from nature, although the reviewer in the *Literary Gazette* commented that its high finish seemed incompatible with a work produced in this way. Since Alfred Stannard was working in Joseph's studio at this time, it does seem likely that Joseph too worked in oil on the spot. Despite their fairly finished quality, it does seem possible that some small pictures such as *Boats on the Yare, Bramerton* (Plate 60) could have been at least begun outdoors, and other more obviously sketch-like works have been attributed to Stannard.

Stannard was not a drawing master, but he did have two pupils, his brother Alfred (1806–89) and the Reverend E. T. Daniell (1804–42). Alfred Stannard taught drawing in Norwich, and painted in a style based essentially on his brother's, but his handling tends to be slicker and more stylized, and his compositions more obviously artificial. Although he was only an amateur, E. T. Daniell was a far more talented artist. Daniell's fame rests mainly on his etchings, although he did produce some magnificent drawings, particularly those of Eastern subjects from the last

70

years of his life. He learnt to etch in Stannard's studio, and his early prints of 1824–8 develop clearly on the tradition of Norwich etching and reflect the influence of Stannard's own. Thereafter he followed a pattern we have seen with other Norwich artists: he lived in the city only intermittently, and absorbed outside influences which transformed his style. His later prints, which suggest contact with Andrew Geddes and other Scottish etchers, are some of the finest painter's etchings to be produced in this country prior to Whistler's.

*

In the 1820s the Norwich Society could still mount an impressive display of local talent. Not only were Stannard, J. B. Crome, Vincent and Stark all exhibiting, but Cotman had returned to the city in 1823, and from then until the exhibitions came to an end in 1833 he showed large numbers of works in almost every year. He was the Society's Vice President in 1831 and 1832, President in 1833, and he also played an active role in organizing the loan exhibitions of 1828–9 and the *conversaziones* of 1830–2, new entertainments through which the artists tried to stimulate a more widespread interest in their activities.

Cotman took a large house that he could ill afford near the Bishop's Palace, and concentrated once again on teaching. His work in watercolour had changed considerably since his early years in Norwich, and many of the drawings he now exhibited were highly coloured views of continental scenery painted in a virtuoso manner. His skies were usually an intense cobalt blue, his buildings a warm yellow with detail drawn in

59. Joseph Stannard (1797–1830): *Yarmouth Sands*. Exhibited 1829?
Oil on panel, 75.2 × 102.9 cm. (29⅝ × 40½ in.) Norwich, Castle Museum

60. Joseph Stannard (1797–1830): *Boats on the Yare, Bramerton, Norfolk*. 1828.
Oil on panel, 57.2 × 77.2 cm. (22½ × 30⅜ in.) Cambridge, Fitzwilliam Museum

brown ink, and his figures picked out in brilliant local colour. These drawings rival Bonington's in their facility and glitter but are still more stylized. Although Cotman was partly inspired by things he had seen on his own continental travels, he was never to go abroad again after 1820, and he had never seen many of the places he now drew. He thus had to rely on prints and drawings by other artists, but the powerful imagination which is also reflected in his literary subjects (Plate 63), often enabled him to completely transform his sources. Like Bonington, Turner and others, Cotman now strengthened his drawings by combining body colour with areas of transparent wash, and by about 1830 he was sometimes mixing flour with his pigments to achieve denser effects. Although Cotman found local buyers for quite a number of these drawings, in Norwich, as in London, they met with a mixed reception. While the Norwich press usually applauded his genius,

61. John Sell Cotman (1782–1842): *Dutch Boats off Yarmouth*. Exhibited 1824.
Oil on panel, 43.5 × 63.5 (17⅛ × 25 in.) Norwich, Castle Museum

both the *Mercury* and the *Chronicle* sometimes found it hard to appreciate the extravagance of his colouring.

In these years Cotman also produced his finest achievements as a painter in oil. Small pictures such as *The Baggage Waggon, The Mishap* and *Silver Birches* (all in the Norwich Castle Museum) clearly show his remarkable appreciation of the sensuous qualities of the medium, and his tremendous gift for pictorial design. *Dutch Boats off Yarmouth* (Plate 61),

exhibited in Norwich in 1824, is an essentially Turnerian conception, but handled with a restraint completely alien to Turner. It is a poetic evocation of a memory, and the picture is full of local associations, for the boats are symbols of British naval triumphs, and in the distance is Yarmouth's monument to the Norfolk hero, Lord Nelson. Although Cotman sold this particular painting at a low price, generally he seems to have had difficulty in selling his oils at all.

62. Joseph Stannard (1797–1830): *Buckenham Ferry, Norfolk. c.*1826.
Pencil and watercolour, 13 × 34.6 cm. (5⅛ × 13⅝ in.) Norwich, Castle Museum

Miles Edmund Cotman (1810–58) began to exhibit a significant number of works after 1828, often with the same or similar subjects to those of his father. At times their style was so close that it is hard to distinguish between their work (Plate 67), but Miles Edmund had an original spirit, and ultimately he did develop a style of his own. Cotman's sons continued to teach drawing in Norfolk after he himself moved to London in 1833 to take up the post of Drawing Master at King's College, and they became important figures in a small circle of amateurs. The extremely talented John Joseph Cotman (1814–78) was to live there intermittently until his death, and produced some of the most remarkable of later Norwich School paintings.

Although the departure of Stark, Cotman and J. B. Crome, and the deaths of Stannard and Vincent must all have contributed to the collapse of the Norwich Society exhibitions, there were other reasons too. In 1826–7 the Society lost its rooms, which were demolished to make way for a new corn exchange. The members had to raise the money to build new premises, and they sent out a circular letter soliciting aid from the propertied classes. The letter commented bluntly on the apathy of Norwich towards its artists, and stated that the exhibitions had consistently run at a loss in recent years and few pictures had been sold from them.

The renewal of the exhibitions in 1828 cost a major effort, and it was probably for this reason that Thirtle began to exhibit again, showing a total of nine works over the years 1828–30. He had produced few finished works since he stopped exhibiting in 1817, and his later drawings were in a new style. They are even more solidly painted and finely observed than those from before 1817, and they create an even stronger illusion of atmosphere. The view of Cromer illustrated in Plate 64 was probably exhibited in 1830, and is one of the best-preserved of his late works. The clouds and atmospheric recession in this are wonder-

74

fully suggested. None of Thirtle's known drawings can be dated after 1830, and he stopped exhibiting again after that year. It is possible that ill health and business commitments forced him to give up painting, although he lived on until 1839.

The collapse of the Society of Artists can be linked with the general decline of the polite amusements in Norwich, and from the early 1830s onwards the *Norwich Mercury* was complaining that the entertainments of Assize Week no longer drew the crowds they once had. However, its demise was not the end of art in the city. It was followed by a number of short-lived societies which organized exhibitions, and artists and amateurs still met at each other's houses and went on sketching parties together. But the general standard of Norwich art does not bear comparison with that from the heady days when Crome and Cotman had lived in the city. The productions of amateurs like Leman and Lound, and particularly their outdoor sketches in watercolour (Plate 65), were often of a surprisingly high quality, but there were no longer any professional artists of sufficient calibre for a school to form around.

John Joseph Cotman was a far more unstable and erratic personality than his father and could never have become the centre of a group. Otherwise the most talented of the later artists were Henry Bright (1810–73) and John Middleton (1827–56). Bright, who came from Saxmundham in Suffolk, was living in Norwich probably from the mid-1820s until 1833, being apprenticed to Alfred Stannard for part of that time. But although he often visited Norwich and sometimes exhibited there, Bright never again lived in the city. Some aspects of Bright's work reflect the influence of the Stannards, and of Leman and Lound, with whom he remained close friends. The view of Yarmouth beach illustrated here (Plate 66) has a fresh spontaneous technique, probably in-

63. John Sell Cotman (1782–1842): *Sir Simon Spruggins, Knt.* Exhibited 1831. Watercolour, 43.8 × 33 cm. (17¼ × 13 in.) Norwich, Castle Museum

64. John Thirtle (1777–1839): *Cromer*. Exhibited 1830? Watercolour, 25.5 × 35.1 cm. (10 × 13¾ in.) London, British Museum

65. Thomas Lound (1802–1861): *Yarmouth Beach*. 1830s?
Watercolour, 12.2 × 18.6 cm. (4¾ × 7¼ in.) London, British Museum

spired by Bonington's oils, but many of his later works have an unpleasantly theatrical quality which is alien to modern taste. A comparison with treatments of this theme by earlier artists (Plates 7, 8, and 59) shows how Bright was moving from the Romantic naturalism of the early Norwich School towards the sentimental mood and superficial mannerisms of so much Victorian landscape painting, and Bright had an extremely successful career. To some extent he did continue to paint Norfolk subjects, but he was equally attracted to many other types of landscape. His pupil John Middleton, who also studied under J. B. Ladbrooke, was a far more interesting artist. Middleton lived in Norwich all his life, but his energies were partly absorbed in running his family's colour business, and he died too young to become any kind of leader.

There is no very obvious reason why a school of painting developed in Norwich in

78

66. Henry Bright (1810–1873): *North Beach, Great Yarmouth*. Early 1840s.
Oil on canvas, 41 × 79.1 cm. (16⅛ × 31⅛ in.) Norwich, Castle Museum

the early nineteenth century. The city was not prosperous, and although local collectors did buy Norwich pictures, at least by the 1820s patrons were in notoriously short supply, so that the artists were increasingly forced to exhibit outside the city. Norwich certainly had a vital intellectual life, but it was probably no richer than that of Liverpool, Bristol or some other cities. Neither was the Society of Artists a particularly remarkable phenomenon. The only thing in fact which seems unique to Norwich is that two of the greatest landscapists of the period chose to live there. Crome and Cotman would probably have been far better off had they taken their chances in London,

but without them no significant art would have come out of Norwich.

The Norwich School has been pitifully represented in the major exhibitions of British Romantic art over the last two decades. It has been described as 'essentially conservative', and there seems to be a widespread misconception that Norwich School pictures were pastiches of Dutch seventeenth-century landscapes produced in the studio. As the illustrations in this book show, Dutch painting was only one of the influences on Norwich artists, and what is more striking is their efforts to transfer the fresh perceptions of their outdoor sketches into finished pictures, and their willingness to absorb the influence of other contemporary landscapists. With the exceptions of Crome and Cotman, none of the Norwich artists were remarkable innovators, but they certainly managed to keep abreast with developments elsewhere.

67. Miles Edmund Cotman (1810-1858): *Interior of a Barn*. 1830s?
Watercolour, 40 × 27.6 cm. (15¾ × 10⅞ in.) Norwich, Castle Museum